When You Meet Your Match: My Match.com Marriage

OUR 10 SECRETS TO A HAPPY MARRIAGE

DEE DEE PATTERSON

When You Meet Your Match: My Match.com Marriage – Our 10 Secrets To A Happy Marriage

When You Meet Your Match: My Match.com Marriage – Our 10 Secrets To A Happy Marriage / Patterson, Dee Dee / Non-Fiction / Self-Help / Relationships / Marriage / Dating

ISBN: 978-1-7360503-0-9

Dedications

For my mom, who died a year before I could publish this book; your death inspired me to finally accomplish my goal of writing a book. I wish you were here to see it.

For my husband, who is the inspiration behind the story, thank you for being an awesome husband.

Acknowledgments

I am grateful for the opportunity to write about my success with Match.com. I love being married and appreciate you for reading my story and tips about having a healthy marriage. I want to acknowledge those who have helped in the creation of this book.

Thank you to my family for your encouragement. Thank you, Aunt Rosalyn, who gave me the courage to publish the book. Thank you to my brother, Winston, for coming up with the title of the book. Thank you to my dad, sister, and cousins for your constant support.

Thank you to my friends for endorsing this book and being amongst the first readers.

Thank you to my editor, Shaundale Rénā, for your excellent editing skills.

Thank you to Match.com for introducing me to my husband.

Finally, thank you to my husband for allowing me to share our story and tell all of our business. I love you, and I love being married to you.

Table of Contents

Introduction

heard marriage was going to be hard. I heard about the 50% divorce rate in the United States, which may or may not be true—people are still debating that number's accuracy. Whatever the actual percentage of failed marriages, it would seem the prospect for a successful marriage is slim.

I've often heard co-workers grudgingly state they have to go home to their spouses and make "jokes" about the tribulations of married life. I also did not have many positive examples of successful marriages in my family. My older relatives stayed together for many years, but only by ignoring or accepting their spouses' infidelity. One aunt told me she was married for four "looong" years, one aunt was married for seven months, and another was married for a week!

A relative told me right before I got married the first year was going to be the hardest, and one of my husband's co-workers gave him a stark warning before our wedding, "Dooon't do it!!!" *Thanks, husband's co-worker.*

Luckily, my husband did not listen to his colleague, and we did get married. After the wedding, I waited and waited for it to get hard. It never did! In fact, marriage has been wonderful. It has been one of the easiest parts of my life. No, seriously, it has been really easy.

I am familiar with hard things. My work life has been hard. Dealing with difficult people and terrible bosses at work has been hard. But, being married has been the bright spot of my life. No matter how terrible of a day at work I've had, I know I will go home to a wonderful husband and spend the rest of the day with him.

Now, I know many people do not feel as I do. Marriage really is hard for them. When these people think of marriage, they think of a challenging situation they have to endure. For some, marriage can be a place of torment and agony. One lady, whose blog I read, said she would rather wrestle a bear or swim with a shark than stay married to her spouse.

Marriage does not have to be that way. It can be one of the best things going for you. From what I have experienced, marriage can provide you a supportive partner with whom to share your life, the foundation to reach your goals faster, and a safe haven from the craziness in this world. Wouldn't you like a spouse to hang onto during the madness?

Marriage can be like you dreamed it would be when you were a little child. It does not have to be the scary way it is portrayed in the movies and on television.

I was pleasantly surprised when I discovered how easy married life could be. I've wanted to tell everyone I knew about how fun being married is, but I didn't want to jinx it. Now that we have been married for 10 years, I think it's safe to share. I want to help others have a good marriage, too, especially those who have been reluctant to get married because of the negative press the institution has received.

I started thinking about what my husband and I do to have such a good marriage and made a list of those things. Then I used that list as the basis for this book. Here, I share our secrets to having a happy marriage. I know marriage is one of those things that can be really good or really miserable. I want your marriage to be one of your "really good" things. Perhaps the things that worked for us can work for you.

As you read this book, you will notice I talk about God a lot. While I will provide you with tips on making your marriage successful, deep down, I know it is my relationship with God and answered prayers that have helped the most in me having a successful marriage. I don't want you to be surprised or put off by the many references to my faith.

This book is really for anyone. If you're already married, you can still use the tips you didn't have to make your marriage better. If you're single, you can start on the right foot, and use the advice provided to ensure you have a terrific marriage. If you're divorced, you can apply what you learn to achieve a better outcome if you marry again.

For those of you who still have a very positive view of marriage, but just can't find a good person to marry, I will also tell how I met my husband on Match.com. I used to be in your shoes. I wanted to be married badly—to have someone to grow old and build a family with. I just couldn't find anyone I wanted to marry. Doing a search on Match.com was the first step in making all of my dreams come true. I will tell you more about how I met my husband online and why I recommend you try online dating to meet your spouse. I will also give you some tips on how to be more successful in finding your spouse online.

Let me start there first. In the next chapter, I will describe the unexpected way I met the man of my dreams and identify the lessons I learned that might help you find your spouse.

Chapter 1

Our Match.com Story

There's a commercial about two people who were ashamed they met online. When one couple asked the two where they met, the two people made up different stories. Then when the two people asked the other couple where they met, the other couple named an online dating site. The two embarrassed people admitted that's where they met too.

This commercial is funny because many people are reluctant to do online dating or admit they met their spouse online; you may think it makes you seem desperate. I was hesitant to do online dating too. I thought I was too good for it. However, when I met my husband, I did not mind telling people how we met because I love our story.

I'm eager to tell you the story, too. I hope it will inspire you to try online dating. After I tell you our story, I will give you tips on how you can safely meet your spouse online as well.

Although my husband and I lived less than 20 miles from each other, I can't think of any other way our paths would have crossed if it hadn't been for online dating. I am grateful to Match.com for introducing us. It might be the way you meet your spouse too. Here's our story.

I had my first free weekend in a long time. I decided to spend my lazy Saturday watching movies on the *Lifetime* channel. If you are not familiar with *Lifetime*, it is a channel geared toward women and usually has women in lead roles. Back then, on Saturdays, *Lifetime* showed back-to-back, captivating two-hour movies for women. It's been a long time since I have had the time to watch a 2-hour *Lifetime* movie, so I'm not sure if the channel still does that on Saturdays.

On that Saturday, it was a week before Labor Day. Match.com had a special going where it was advertising a free communications week for visitors to the site. At first, I ignored the commercials. I tried online dating many years before and had negative experiences. I only met one guy in person. He did not look like he did in his picture, and there was absolutely no chemistry. I also talked to a few men on the phone. Eventually, we stopped calling each other, and that was it.

When I kept seeing the Match.com commercial, it annoyed me. Back then, if you stayed on a channel too long, you would see the same commercials over and over again. Since I spent the day watching *Lifetime* movies, I probably saw the Match.com commercial at least 10 times. The commercials kept saying the same thing over and over again; *it's okay to look. It's okay to look.* Finally, late in the evening, I decided to look. My purpose was to prove Match.com didn't work.

I did a very specific search of what would be the perfect guy for me. I searched for things like height over 6 feet, age range around mine, no drinking, no smoking, lived within 20 miles of me, never married, and no children.

After selecting the precise criteria, I clicked search and waited for the results. When I got the results, I was shocked. One person met my criteria. I couldn't believe it. I stared back at the picture; I was very attracted to him. Under his image, it said active within the last 24 hours. That scared me a little bit. *This guy is probably already talking to someone,* I thought.

I also read the description next to his picture, and he mentioned his Christian faith. I really wanted to meet him, but I didn't want to make the first move. By then, it was late, so I went to sleep with Match.com guy on my mind.

At church the next day, I constantly thought about the mystery guy. After church, I went to a life group, a small group for church members to meet and discuss topics together. I was a member of the singles life group, but I have no idea what we talked about that day. I remember someone asking me if everything was okay because I seemed distracted. I mentioned the guy online, but I don't remember going into any details.

At home that evening, I called my brother and sister. I had a really close relationship with them and asked them separately if I should send the guy a message.

They both said yes. My sister helped me craft the message. It basically said something about me doing a specific search on Match.com, and he was the only one who met the criteria. It ended with a question about whether he was interested in getting to know me.

When I woke up Monday morning, I was very excited when I saw I had a message from the guy. He said he was interested in getting to know me and asked me questions about myself. We went back and forth in email throughout the day. Then we moved to texting. I definitely did not earn my 8-hour salary at work that day. By the end of the workday, he said he was going to call me that evening.

At home, I was so anxious for his call that I had to keep myself busy. When he finally called me, the conversation went very well. It flowed nicely, and we planned our first date for that Wednesday evening at a restaurant.

On Tuesday, we talked on the phone again. Then on Wednesday, we met for the first time as planned. He arrived at the restaurant first, and I parked my car next to his.

When he got out of his car, I was still happy to be attracted to him. In our conversations, he made it seem like he was obese. He kept trying to warn me about his size, so I worried a little that he was too big for my taste, but I was relieved when I saw him.

His size, height, and weight were perfect for me. He was very handsome. I couldn't help but give him a spontaneous hug. Afterward, I felt a little embarrassed that I was making the first move again, but I couldn't help it. We had talked on the phone for the last few days and really got to know each other. For me to be attracted to him physically, as well as mentally, was a big plus.

In the restaurant, we had good conversations. We got a deal where we could order an appetizer and a dessert with our meal. We easily agreed on barbecue wings for the appetizer and apple pie for the dessert.

After we finished eating, things got interesting. When we walked to our cars, this time, my date initiated the hug. It felt incredible. It was a nice, warm, bear hug. Apparently, my future husband liked the hug, too, because he didn't let go of me. We just stood in the restaurant parking lot, holding each other.

Finally, I looked up, and he met me with a kiss. We kissed for a long time. It wasn't until a couple in the restaurant came out and reacted to us kissing in the middle of the parking lot that we stopped. I don't curse, but the guy yelled out a four-letter word that starts with a "D." I jumped away from my date. I told him I had to go and went to my car. He pulled me out of my car, and we hugged and kissed again. Eventually, we finally got into our separate cars and left.

My sister called as I was driving home. She asked me how the date went, and I remember telling her, "It was magical." The whole date caught me off guard. I didn't expect to feel so much chemistry. It was an amazing feeling.

After that first date, things moved pretty fast with my future husband and me. We had our second date that Saturday. We talked to each other on the phone or saw each other in person every day after that first date.

We met each other's family quickly. I met his sister and niece within a few weeks of us dating; my grandmother was the first family member he met of mine. Within a month, we were saying we loved each other. My parents visited for Thanksgiving and met him. We lived down south, and my parents lived up north. For Christmas, we drove 800 miles to my hometown and stayed with them. We stopped and visited my brother on the way. There was a universal feeling from everyone that he was the right guy for me. My grandma even called me after she met him and said, "You hit the jackpot."

My husband proposed to me eight months after we met, and we married a year and two days after we first met in person. We got married on August 28 or 8/28. I loved the date because it reminds me of my favorite Bible verse Romans 8:28, "And we know that all things work together for good to those who love God, to those who are the called according to his purpose."

So, that's our story. Ten years later, we're still together and living in happy marital bliss. Now let me discuss some tips for online dating that will help you meet your spouse.

Online Dating Tips:

- Be Proactive

- Be Safe

- Be Honest

- Be Patient

Be Proactive

First, if you see someone you are interested in online, you should go ahead and make the first move. If I did not send a message first, I might have never met my husband. Although you may be afraid of getting rejected, you should make the first move anyway; like my husband, the person may be interested in getting to know you. If the person is not interested in you, good. You will know that's not the right person for you.

I grew up in a church listening to preachers who said a woman should not look for a husband; the husband finds the wife. Preachers used the scripture, Proverbs

18:22. According to the New King James Version of the Bible, "*He who* finds a wife finds a good *thing* and obtains favor from the LORD."

When I got older, I studied the scripture myself. I realized the verse emphasizes the idea of having a wife. The scripture is not emphasizing how the person found the wife. It is not saying only the man should do the looking; it's saying it's a good thing for him who gets a wife. It was liberating to know I did not necessarily have to wait for the guy to find me. If I never sent that email to my future husband, I could have missed out on being in a happy marriage.

My advice to a male or a female wanting to be married is to go after what you want. If not, nothing will happen. You have to put yourself out there. You may face disappointments. If so, don't give up. Don't let your shyness or fear of rejection hold you back from your dreams of getting married.

You might believe that you will meet your spouse in your everyday daily experiences. If you have not met your spouse at work or church yet, you might have to do something differently. Going online expanded my choices of men, and it can provide you with more options too.

Be Safe

While I lucked out and met a really good guy online, I know there are crazy people out there. You have to be safe when meeting someone in person. One thing I did when I first started talking to my husband was to verify the information he provided. You can do a lot of free online searches to verify who you are talking to. I did a quick Google search to make sure he came up when I looked him up.

His social media came up, but his name did not. I realized he did not use his real name. I asked him what his real name is, and then I found him easily online. I was able to verify he lived in his current city and the hometown where he used to live. I also could verify his age. If any of the information you find online does not match what the person says, ask clarifying questions in a non-accusatory way. For instance, "Did you say you grew up in (name the state)?" Or, "Have you ever lived in (name the state)?"

If the information online still does not match what the person tells you, consider not building a relationship with him or her. It is important to weed out the liars early on. You can't build a strong, healthy marriage with someone who lies all of the time.

Although I did not meet him online, I dated someone who lied a lot. Once I knew he was a liar, I asked him questions I already knew the answers to. I wanted to see how he would respond. Of course, his responses were always a lie. The relationship did not last much longer because I realized he was a smooth-talking liar.

You should want someone honest. My husband was very honest when we were dating and continues to be. I liked that he told me the truth even when he knew I wouldn't like the answer. I valued the fact that he was honest over being upset at the negative information he told me.

Other people might want to weed out people with significant criminal backgrounds. In some states, there are free online websites where you can check the person's criminal records or anytime the person had to go to court. In my state, it is the state name and "judiciary case search."

If the person does not have a criminal background, then you're good. Make sure you have the person's correct first and last name. If the crime is minor, don't worry about it. Someone getting a speeding ticket should not be a deal-breaker. If the person does have a criminal background and you have a good feeling about them, you could still cautiously move forward with them. It may work out because people do change.

If you find any questionably severe information about someone you're interested in, move on. If you see anything dealing with violence or sexual crimes, it should be a no-go. There are plenty of honest, trustworthy people online who are looking for a good spouse.

While some may call this stalking, think of it as research for safety reasons. I know some of this safety talk might have scared you from online dating. There's a small chance of you meeting a crazy person. Verifying the person's information reduces the risk. Also, talking to the person on the phone lets you know if you want to meet in person.

The small risks are worth it if you take precautions, and there's a chance you might meet your potential spouse.

Another way to be safe is to meet the person in a public location on the first date. I met my future husband at a restaurant where there were cameras and plenty of people around. We drove separate cars to get there. If I didn't like my husband, I could have gotten in my car and gone home without any issues.

If you have a bad date, you don't have to see the person again. Don't string the person along. When you talk to each other again, let the person know you are no longer interested in dating. Then move on. You should not waste time on someone you know you do not want to marry.

Be Honest

If you are looking for someone you want to spend your life with, you have to put accurate information on your profile. Use your real picture, put your actual age, and write an accurate description of yourself. Again, you should not start your relationship off with lies. The only way you can attract someone right for you is if you accurately present yourself.

You do not have to put your life story in your description. The shorter the description of yourself, the better. Having too many details may be intimidating. Save your details for the potential people you talk to on the phone.

Be Patient

You will probably not match up with your first connection. It does not mean you should give up. Give yourself some time to meet the right person.

My husband actually paid for a month's membership. When he first got on Match.com, he sent messages to women and never got any traction. Then he stopped being active and was going to let his membership expire. I got on Match.com three weeks later and found his profile, and we ended up being compatible. His profile would have expired a week after I got on. I'm so glad he was still on Match.com, and I got to meet him.

Be patient. Your future spouse may not get on Match.com the exact same time you do, so don't give up so easily. Continue to browse profiles. Another thing you need to be patient about is the relationship. My husband and I did too much too soon on our first date. Either the second or third date, we realized we needed to slow down and really get to know each other in a non-physical way.

Being patient worked for us. We were able to consummate our marriage on our wedding day. Consider not getting physical with your date too soon. It may cloud your judgment on whether the person is really the right one for you. Also, once you get married, you will have a lifetime to physically enjoy your spouse.

Hopefully, these tips will help with online dating. The rest of the chapters are secrets to having a happy marriage. The first point is the best advice for having a successful union.

Chapter 2

Tip #1: Choose the Right Person

Shortly after I went ring shopping with my boyfriend, I begin to panic. Many thoughts raced through my head. *He's not what I pictured my future husband to be like. Do I really want to spend the rest of my life with him? He only has a few of the qualities I wanted in a man. Why would God make me wait so long to get married, and it be to a guy who only had a few of the qualities I wanted?*

It was that last question that helped me make my decision. I broke up with my boyfriend soon after we went ring shopping. Three weeks later, I met my husband online. I have no regrets about my decision. I chose the right person to marry.

Choosing the right person is the easiest, best way to have a happy marriage. I could end the book on this one line. Make sure you choose the right person. This advice is for single and divorced readers who want to get married/remarried. If you believe you may not have chosen the right person and you are married, I am not advocating for you to end your marriage. Instead, some of the other tips in this book may be useful to improve your relationship.

I know it is tough to find the right person to marry. Don't settle. It is hard to thrive and reach your fullest potential, married to the wrong person. If I married my ex-boyfriend and did not wait for my now-husband, I know I would be miserable. I'm glad I expected the best from God and waited for the man who had the qualities I desired. I believe God rewarded me for trusting in Him.

You are probably wondering *how do you know if someone is the right person*? The first thing you should do is trust your gut. I had a sinking feeling with my ex-boyfriend that I should not marry him. If you are having feelings of doubt about getting married to your partner, trust yourself.

You may or may not know why you are having doubts. Still, you should trust your instincts. With my husband, I had no doubts he was the right guy for me. On our wedding day, I was very relaxed about the idea of marrying him. He said he felt the same way about marrying me.

Another sign to look for is how well the relationship is going. When my husband and I were dating, our relationship was straightforward. My husband described the relationship as "natural." We got along very well. We did not have a lot of drama and huge fights. If your relationship is messy, that person is probably not the right one for you. You do not want a WWE type of marriage where you are fighting all of the time.

I had other relationships in the past that were very awkward, and we had trouble keeping a conversation going. If you can't communicate easily with the person, you probably should not get married.

Another way to know is to picture yourself spending the rest of your life with the person. I ended relationships with men because they had habits I knew I could not live with forever. For my husband, I liked him just the way he was without him having to change anything. You should feel the same way about your future spouse. You could live with the person for the rest of your life, even if that person does not change.

Sometimes, when we are with someone, we fall in love with who they could be, not who they are currently. The person is not guaranteed to change. You could be very disappointed if you marry a person, expecting them to change. The way the person is before you get married will be the same person after marriage. Marry someone you like in their current version.

I like something my uncle said to me when I was single. He told me that two whole people should get married. He meant people should be whole by themselves before marriage, not need someone to make them whole.

My husband and I were both living in our own places. We both had jobs and were paying bills on our own before we got married. We didn't need each other to survive. We were making a living on our own. Some people get in relationships with people who are dependent on them. These people like to feel needed. Having someone who depends on you can be cute at first, but it will get old quickly. You will want someone who is your partner and who is a strong contributor to the relationship.

Along the same line of thought, be wary of people who ask you for money too soon in the dating relationship, especially to pay their bills. How were they paying their bills before you? It will be difficult for you to tell if you are really in a loving relationship or if the person is interested in you for what you can give them.

I mistakenly gave money to a guy I was dating. Early in the relationship, he kept asking me for a loan to start a business and said he would share the proceeds. I was buying a house, so he knew my credit was good. I kept saying I didn't feel comfortable signing a loan for him. I was just tired of him asking me and agreed to do it to stop him from bothering me. As you can guess, he disappeared soon after I signed the loan for him, and I was stuck with the payment. He did end up starting the business, but I never saw a dime of his profits—more about this story in a later chapter.

I should have ended the relationship when he first started asking for money. I should have known then that I did not want to marry a guy who would ask me for money early in our dating relationship. Don't get me wrong; I think it is fine to spend money on your partner during a date. You can decide who pays for dates or take turns. It can be challenging for one person to pay for all of the dates if you are dating for a long time. However, I believe, when it comes to personal living expenses, you should be able to hold your own when you are single.

After marriage, it is a different story. One of the later chapters discusses how my husband and I successfully manage our money together. Since being married, we have doubled and almost tripled our household income. In that chapter, I will let you know how we did it.

Besides being independent with money, make sure your partner is emotionally stable. If your partner still needs to heal from a bad breakup or a traumatic situation, the person may not be ready for marriage yet. They still need to grow as a person or get help before getting married. Otherwise, they will bring some of that trauma into the marriage. Look for signs that the person is not emotionally ready to get married yet.

If you have situations you still need to heal from, work on getting whole before looking for a spouse. Marriage works best when there are two emotionally healthy people joined together. After I graduated from college, I thought I was ready to get married. It wasn't until four years later that I met my husband. In the meantime, I bought a house, learned to pay my own bills, and how to fend for myself. I grew more confident and really got to know myself. Being alone and independent helped me to be ready once I met my husband. I was definitely a stronger, more secure person when it was time to get married.

A final way to know if your partner is the one is how the person treats you. You should feel special when you are around them. You should feel like the person only has eyes for you. I was sitting near a guy who turned and looked at every female who walked by him. I was not dating him, but it made me feel uncomfortable.

You will want a partner who is content with only being with you. When you first start dating, you may be dating more than one person. Once the relationship gets serious, the two of you should only be dating each other. Both my husband and I had to tell our exes to stop calling. We were serious about our relationship and did not want any distractions.

The person you marry should treat you with respect, and you should feel good being around them. If they always make you upset, that person may not be the right one. If they negatively talk about you, then that's not someone who will enhance your life.

You should love the person you marry and have feelings for them. The person should feel the same way about you. Some people consider marrying out of convenience. It is not likely to last. You need to have strong feelings of love for the person. It will help the marriage to survive any obstacle that comes.

Think about all of these characteristics when you are trying to decide if the person you are in a relationship with is the person you should marry. Choosing the right person is essential in having a happy marriage.

In the next chapter, I will discuss something you should do before you get married to bolster your future marriage.

Chapter 3

Tip #2: Get Pre-marital Counseling

When I was in school, I liked the teachers who provided a comprehensive review before a big test. The teachers would go over all of the possible questions that may show up, then provide the answers to the items or showed us how to get to the right response. The teacher would work with us in any areas where we were weak and answer our questions until we felt confident that we could answer a question on the test dealing with the topic.

The way a teacher gets you ready for a big test reminds me of how pre-marital counseling prepares you for marriage. If you are not married already, I recommend getting pre-marital counseling beforehand. I believe pre-marital counseling helped me and my husband to build our marriage on a strong foundation.

One 2006 study in the *Journal of Family Psychology* shows that pre-marital education participation results in higher marital satisfaction levels and lower levels of destructive conflicts. The research also indicates that pre-marital education resulted in a 31% decrease in divorce odds.

Both my husband and I wanted to go to pre-marital counseling before we got married. I wanted to go because I met this dude on the Internet. I wanted to make sure what we had was real. The pre-marital counseling confirmed that we were right for each other. We got the highest level of compatibility for the test we took.

When we met, we went to different churches and wanted to see what each church had to offer. The assistant minister at my church readily agreed to conduct pre-marital counseling for us. We kept calling my husband's church to see if we could get pre-marital counseling, but we could never reach anyone. My church won. We decided to go with that assistant minister.

Since it has been about 10 years, I don't remember everything about pre-marital counseling. I think we had three sessions that were each one hour. We might have received a shortened pre-marital session since we scheduled the wedding four months after getting engaged. The normal sessions might double that, about 6 to 10 meetings.

The following is is how our pre-marital counseling sessions went. Before our first session, my husband and I each took the Prepare/Enrich online assessment. The assessment has been the #1 Pre-marital and Marriage Assessment for over 35 years, according to the Prepare/Enrich website. The cost is currently $35 per couple; I don't remember how much it was back then. We only paid for the evaluation, as we did not have to pay the assistant minister for the accompanying counseling sessions.

We discussed the test results at our three sessions and reviewed topics such as communication, conflict resolution, habits, financial management, relationship roles, children and parenting, and spiritual beliefs. The sessions were good because these were topics we didn't discuss in depth before we got engaged. All we knew is that we loved each other and wanted to get married. It was good that the assistant minister gave us a reality check and addressed these issues with us.

One topic that had the most significant impact on me was conflict resolution. The assistant minister pointed out when we had different answers on the Prepare/Enrich assessment. Conflict resolution was one of those areas.

When we were dating, my husband tended to give in to what I wanted. We discussed with the assistant minister why he did that. My husband told him that he dealt with people arguing in his past, and he thought someone should have given in and end the argument. I told the assistant minister I would rather my husband defend his side instead of easily giving in.

That discussion before we got married was very enlightening to me. When we did get married and had a disagreement, I remembered it. Whenever my husband tried to avoid conflict and just give in to what I wanted, I asked him what he thought. Then I would listen to his reasoning, and most of the time, our solution would be a combination of both of our thoughts. Other times he had the best solution, and I am glad we went with his suggestion. In later chapters, I will discuss in more detail about us healthily resolving conflict for discussions such as finding a house and whether or not to circumcise our son.

I am grateful to pre-marital counseling for allowing us to discuss our methods of resolving conflict before we got married. It probably prevented my husband from having resentment toward me. I can't imagine anyone liking it if one partner always gets their way. Yet, there are marriages where one partner always ends up winning every argument to the other partner's detriment.

Some people are peacemakers and like to get issues resolved quickly. That may result in the person letting the other person have their way. I didn't realize the reasoning behind my husband agreeing with my decisions until we went to pre-marital counseling. I realize now that he was not completely happy with every decision we made. It motivated me to make sure we both agree on the decisions we were making moving forward.

My husband tended to be more passive, and I can be assertive sometimes. (Okay, I can be assertive a lot of times.) Usually, there is one partner who is a little more assertive than the other. The odds of both partners having the exact same personality is pretty slim. If you're the partner who always gets your way, try to be more accommodating. Eventually, it will get old that your partner always yields to your demands. It will cause resentment to build up. Try to make sure your relationship is mutually beneficial and satisfying to both parties involved. A marriage cannot be successful if one of the partners is selfish.

If you play the peacemaker role and are always sacrificing, let your partner know you want things to be more even. Don't wait until you are fed up and yelling or emotional; find a good time when you're both calm and in a cheerful mood to share what you have been feeling. The partner should want to make sure you are happy too. They may not even realize the relationship is unbalanced. If that doesn't work and you're in the dating stage, you may have to reconsider being in the relationship.

You probably don't want to be married to a controlling person. That goes back to what I said earlier about two whole people getting married. The person is not mature enough to realize a relationship is a balance of two people's thoughts and opinions. They cannot have their way all of the time. If you are already married to a selfish and controlling person, the solution is more complicated. I witnessed a marriage where the husband was very sweet and passive; he always yielded to the wife's demands. The wife did not appreciate it and became more controlling. I kept thinking the husband should have stopped yielding to his wife's demands.

If you are always the one sacrificing, you have to stop doing it. Your partner cannot make you follow their way all the time. The only way the person can do that is if the person uses a weapon or violence. If so, law enforcement needs to be involved. You have to set boundaries and not let the person run over you. The person is more likely to change if you set boundaries than if you continue to let them control you.

Let the person know about your limits and disengage if they try to cross your boundaries. That means you should do things such as walk away or get off the phone with them. I had to learn to do that with the controlling person I knew. I disengaged when they tried to be controlling. It sends the message that you are not going to accept the controlling behavior. Eventually, the person will realize you will not accept getting treated that way. If the person decides to change, it will more likely happen gradually and not overnight. Don't expect a quick fix. Again, the best plan is not to marry a controlling person in the first place. Don't ignore signs that the person you're in a relationship with always has to have it their way.

That's why I am a big advocate of premarital counseling; skeletons can come out of the closet before you get married. My husband and I had several healthy discussions with my assistant minister. I was able to see areas where I needed to do things differently. By the time we got married, I had made the adjustments, contributing to our happy marriage.

As I said earlier, at the end of the premarital counseling, the assistant minister confirmed that my husband and I were ready for marriage. Again, we received the highest level of compatibility with the Prepare/Enrich test. We were considered a Vitalized Couple, which revealed high relationship satisfaction and positive couple agreement scores across most categories. It is the coupling type that is least likely to divorce. Of the four categories, the couple most likely to get a divorce is the Conflicted Couple, which showed low scores across almost all categories. They called this type "Conflicted Couple" because they were still planning to get married despite having relationship difficulties.

Couples should use pre-marital counseling as an opportunity to discuss relevant marriage topics and decide if they should get married in the first place. It's okay to decide you are not ready yet. You may prevent a lot of pain and misery. You want to feel confident that you are making the right decision. After my husband and I received high compatibility scores, I was sure I was ready to get married.

While we discussed several helpful topics during pre-marital counseling, conflict resolution left a lasting impression. Another area of emphasis was financial management. The money activity we did laid the foundation for a financially secure marriage. We will discuss that activity in our next chapter about money, and you will also find out how we could pay cash for most big-ticket items and almost tripled our household income from when we first got married.

Chapter 4

Tip #3: Put Money Together

When I was in my senior year of high school, a lady from a credit card company called to offer me my first credit card. I heard credit cards were not good for you, but I did not have the confidence to say I'm not interested and hang up the phone. (I have no problem doing that now, by the way.) Instead, I provided the details of all of my personal information over the phone. Thank goodness she wasn't a scam artist.

When the credit card arrived in the mail, my mom was mad at me for getting one. I told her I didn't know how to hang up on the lady and assured her I wasn't going to use it. Instead, I put it on my bookshelf, next to my track running trophies, and admired it as a souvenir.

One day the family needed money, and my mom asked me for the credit card. It became the family credit card for unexpected expenses. Mom paid the minimum payments, and when she got a windfall during my sophomore year of college, she paid off the nearly $14,000 owed.

Paying off that credit card left me with a strong credit score. I appreciate my mom for keeping her word and paying me back. Fast forward to when I was living on my own and dating the guy who kept asking me for money. First, we went to a bank, which said they would not give us a loan to start a business. Then the guy asked if I had any more credit. I told him I had a credit card with a $14,000 limit and nothing on it. *Yes, I told him that.* Then we went to a lawnmower store and bought a lawnmower and equipment for the business. Our relationship ended soon after I purchased the equipment. I called him every month to beg him to make a payment on the credit card. Eventually, I lost track of him and had to pay the rest of the balance off myself.

I tell this story to show you how clueless I was about money. I didn't grow up knowing about best practices with finances. I didn't save a lot of money when I had summer internships in college. I didn't inherit a whole bunch of money. I was not skilled in credit card usage. I made many careless mistakes when it came to money. I wanted you to know my beginning mindset regarding finances before I describe how my husband and I handled funds during our marriage. If you have trouble managing your finances, you can start now to improve them. My husband and I knew very little but have since shifted to having no debt besides our mortgage.

Let me start by going back to pre-marital counseling. One of our assistant minister's activities was to make a list of all our debt and the interest rates associated with each one. That was an informative activity. It seems obvious that we should have already made a list, but the thought never occurred to me. I was focused on love and planning the wedding. I appreciated this activity, however. I learned about all of my husband's debt, and he learned about mine.

I can't remember how much debt we had, and I didn't document the number anywhere. I feel as if the number was less than $50,000. We did not have any student loans from college. I had a full academic scholarship to undergraduate school and a full scholarship to my first year of graduate school. I only had a loan of $3,000 from my second year of graduate school that I paid off before I met him. My husband did not go to college. He went to work right after high school. Our loans included both of our car loans, and we each had personal loans. I also still had about $5,000 left from paying for the lawn equipment for the guy I was dating.

After we made our list of debts, my husband discovered one of his loans had a 32% interest rate. I was impressed with him because the next day, he went to a credit union and transferred the loan, getting a 9% interest rate. Our next assignment, armed with our debt list, was to set a budget. We definitely would not have done all of this in advance if it weren't for pre-marital counseling. It also caused us to be more cautious about how much money we spent on our wedding. We had a very cheap church wedding that cost around $5,000. We opened our eyes once we knew how much debt we had.

I recommend couples who are engaged also list their debt and interest rates as we did. It was a very enlightening experience and helped us reach our money goals faster. After we got married, we focused on getting out of debt as soon as possible. We got a joint checking and savings account and deposited our paychecks directly into our joint checking account.

This is the next tip for having a happy marriage: put your money together. To do that, you have to follow the first tip, *Choose the Right Person*. You do not want to put your money together with the wrong person. If you marry someone you trust and is honest, you should feel completely comfortable putting your money together.

In case you missed it, we did not put our money together until after we were married. I recommend not combining your money until after it is official. My husband and I did the planning before we got married, but did not set up actual joint accounts until after the wedding. He moved into my little 3-bed, 2-bath house. It was sort of a windfall for me; I was barely making it on my own. With my husband living with me, there was a second income to pay bills, and he made about $14,000 more a year than me. Still, with the extra income, our focus was on paying off our debt. I forgot to mention the debt did not include the mortgage on the house. We knew we were going to sell the house as soon as we could.

By focusing on our finances, we ended up paying off our debt in 18 months and spent the rest of our marriage debt-free except for the mortgage on our new house. Here's how we did it. Some people focus on debts with the highest interest rates. We decided to focus on the amount of the debts owed. The amount of my husband's car loan and personal loans were lower than my debt. We used all of our extra money and dedicated it to his car loan first. Once we paid off that car loan, we used the extra money to pay off his personal loan. Some people may refer to it as the snowball effect. We kept throwing all of our extra money onto each of our debts until we were debt-free in less than two years.

The nice thing about paying off debt is you have extra money after your bills are paid even if your salary does not increase. After paying off our debt, we started to put all of our extra money into our savings account and built an emergency fund. When we were ready to sell my house, the appraisal returned lower than the amount we asked for. It hurt plenty, but since we had a buyer already, we were willing to pay the $10,000 in cash to get rid of the house to cover closing and any additional costs. Because we were saving so much of our money, we could afford to pay the difference, and it was worth not having to worry about the house anymore.

After we sold my house, we really were debt-free. It put us in a great position for when we found a place we wanted to buy together. We rented a townhouse until we could locate our dream house. Before discussing our forever home search, let me share more of how we do our joint accounts. When we get our money direct deposited into the joint account, we use that account to pay all of our bills, meals at home, gas for both cars, and anything we need for the house.

We do give ourselves money from our paychecks that go to our personal accounts. The money in those accounts goes toward personal items such as clothes, food we have at work, and anything we want to only buy for ourselves. There's not much I spend only for myself, so I save most of that money. It's a no-questions-asked account where we purchase whatever we want for ourselves.

I wanted to note that we put the same amount into both of our personal accounts every month. One partner does not get more in their personal account. I know some financial gurus suggest couples put a percentage in the joint account based on each person's salary, and then the partners keep the rest for themselves. We don't do it that way. We put everything in the joint account and have a set amount in our personal accounts; it has worked very well for us.

We both work hard to increase the amount of money we put into our joint accounts. Before we had children, my husband worked a double every Saturday for a year to increase the money in our accounts. I also worked a shift work position for a year to put the extra pay for working nights and weekends into our accounts. When we get bonuses or raises, we put it in our joint account. We praise each other when we get promotions or pay increases. It's not a competition since all of the extra money goes into our joint accounts.

Most of the time, we pay for big-ticket items out of the joint account. We have many discussions about money. If my husband or I want something, we discuss it, look at the budget, and usually pay for it with cash. We paid cash for cell phones, smart TVs, laptops, our minivan, dishwasher, refrigerator, washer, dryer, finishing our basement, and more.

That's why I recommend putting your money together. You'll be able to get out of debt faster, save more, and pay cash for the things you want. Working together helps our marriage grow stronger. We do not deal with fights about money. We have the same goal to continue to build our savings. For big-ticket items, we both have to agree with the purchase before we buy it. We don't sneak around and buy something from the joint account without letting the other partner know. My husband is usually the one who does all of the research for an item. Once he shows me what we should buy, we often have the money and can afford to get it. If we don't have the money yet, we save until we can comfortably afford to buy it.

That's what we did with our house. We saved up for a down payment on a house while we rented a townhouse. When we were house hunting, my husband was undeniably pickier than me in choosing. I grew up in a condominium, so every single-family house we saw looked good to me. My husband only wanted places with at least 3,000 square feet. I was worried about being house poor. I did not want to buy too big of a house that we couldn't afford to live comfortably. We discussed how we each felt about the house. We knew we were not going to buy unless we both agreed.

When my husband found the house we eventually bought, I told him I didn't like it because it was too big and expensive. We kept looking for places, and then the price dropped on my husband's dream house by

$20,000. We made an offer, and it was accepted. I liked the process we went through because we understood what each of us wanted. The house at 3,500 square feet was big enough to please my husband. When the price dropped, we could get a loan at a good interest rate without paying private mortgage insurance (PMI), which worked for me. We could comfortably afford the house. We made sure both of our needs were satisfied. It really was the best house to meet our needs. To put the icing on the cake, God blessed both of us with promotions the year we bought our house so we could definitely afford it.

My husband and I continue to encourage each other to go for promotions and apply to new jobs. Because we support each other's career growth, we doubled our household income from when we first got married. My personal income has tripled since we got married. In a later chapter, I will talk about my husband's role in helping me get higher-paying jobs.

The message for this chapter is to work together as a team when it comes to finances. Pay off debt together and then save and spend your money smartly together. I know many couples use separate accounts. I believe that combining your money will actually have the best benefits for both of you.

Handling finances together requires constant communication with your spouse. In the next chapter, I will discuss how open communication is crucial to having a happy marriage.

Chapter 5

Tip #4: Communicate Openly

After my husband and I moved in together, I did dishes the first two days. On the third day, I decided to leave the dishes for my husband. I let the dishes pile in the sink so he could see the dishes and wash them. That did not happen. The dishes kept piling up. Finally, after a few days, I told my husband what I was doing. I was leaving the dishes for him. I wanted both of us to share in the household chores.

My husband responded that he didn't know I wanted him to do the dishes, and he didn't know how to use my dishwasher. His response surprised me. I had made up in my head why I thought he did not do the dishes. I thought he wanted me to do all of the cooking and cleaning, even though we both worked fulltime.

I learned a few things about communicating with my husband after that conversation. First, I realized he could not *and cannot* read my mind. Secondly, we do not think alike, so it is necessary to communicate my feelings openly. He does not know what I think unless I tell him. Giving hints and being passive-aggressive does not work; I have to verbally share my thoughts with him. Learning early in our marriage to communicate openly has helped us to have a happy marriage.

A study of 886 divorcing couples in Minnesota revealed 53% of the couples cited an inability to talk together as reasons for marital breakdown. The research shows that open communication is crucial in having a strong marriage.

Over time, my husband and I have improved our communication skills. We usually do not have conversations in the heat of the moment. We wait until a little time has passed, and we are not agitated. It has worked well for us to drop conversations and then discuss each other's side when we are in a better mood. If neither of us is upset, we go ahead and calmly discuss each side when an issue arises. I can think of only a few times when we raised our voices, and the conversation was very heated. We did not accomplish much during those talks.

I recommend that you do not talk to your partner when you are angry. You might say something you regret. You should walk away and wait for a time to talk when you are both calm. You will get more out of the conversation that way. You should always listen to your partner's side of the conversation. Sometimes we can listen to respond with our own agenda and not really listen to hear the other person's perspective. You might be focused on proving you are right or winning the conversation. The focus, instead, should be how you can move forward together on the issue-at-hand.

That reminds me of a weird topic that my husband and I discussed after our son was born. I learned a lot from the conversation, so I am going to tell you the story. We had two daughters first, and our third child was a boy. While growing up, I always thought that when my son was born, he would get circumcised. I told you it was a weird topic. When I read through the Bible, men who were not circumcised were considered "unclean." I did not want my son considered unclean.

After we had the baby and the nurse asked us if we would get *our son* circumcised, I said I wanted to, but we had not talked about it. When the nurse left, my husband asked why I wanted the circumcision. I told him men in the Bible were circumcised. I also told him it was a tradition; the men in my family were also circumcised. When I called around to verify that statement, I found out that none of the men in my immediate family were circumcised. *Oops.*

We asked the nurse to come back and questioned her profusely. I could tell she was being cautious with her language. She said people get their sons circumcised for religious reasons, but hinted that there wasn't really a strong health reason for it. She also said people do it for cosmetic reasons. Then, the male nurse-in-training told my husband a belief that men who are not circumcised feel more pleasure down there. That confirmed it for my husband; he was not in favor of circumcision but left the decision up to me. He was also worried about our son's safety.

I did a quick search on Google and saw no strong reason for circumcision, other than religious purposes. Besides, I was still in a lot of pain from the delivery and did not want to deal with our son being in pain, too. I told my husband I agreed our son should not get circumcised, and he was surprised.

That conversation made me realize that sometimes we have long-held beliefs, not based on facts. I thought the men in my family were circumcised, and it was something all men had to do for health reasons. My husband did not have long-held beliefs and questioned my logic. When he did, it made me consider another perspective.

I appreciate my husband having a different point of view. We grew up with different family backgrounds in different areas of the country. I often think my way is the right way. I hung out with family and friends who validated my same beliefs. When I have conversations with my husband, I like getting his viewpoint. When we are trying to decide, the way forward is based on our combined best ideas.

I think of my husband's views as a benefit and not an obstacle. When we communicate with each other, I learn I'm not always right. *I know, shocking.* That's why we communicate so well with each other. Our conversations are a way for me to learn more about him and what he thinks. Many times, my thinking is entirely different.

My main point in all of this is to urge you to communicate with your spouse as a learning experience. Don't think of it as a battle. Try to understand their perspective. Then make decisions together in a way that will benefit both of you.

I would have never experienced many television shows, movies, or places if it were not for my husband. I had my idea of what I liked. He opened my mind to experience other things. Think of your marriage as a partnership and share ideas with one another.

As I discussed in the chapter on pre-marital counseling, don't let your marriage be one-sided where only one partner benefits. It will be stronger if you both communicate your thoughts and opinions. Create an environment where your spouse feels comfortable sharing ideas. The way I do it is by asking my husband what he thinks about a situation. Then I ask more questions to gain a better understanding of his perspective.

My husband does not easily express his feelings, so I try to create an environment where he does not feel guarded or self-conscious about sharing his thoughts. I can tell when something is bothering him because he gets quieter than usual. I will ask him what is bothering him a few times, and he usually says, "nothing." Then later in the evening or the next day, he will tell me. Then we discuss the issue. I feel good because he eventually feels comfortable enough to let me know about his concerns. Instead of holding them in, I am sure expressing his thoughts feels just as good for him.

When the situation is reversed, I like when he asks what is bothering me. Then he listens when I describe what is on my mind. He usually offers a validating comment to make me feel better. Sometimes he does not even have to ask me what is bothering me. He just asks me how my day went, and everything that is bothering me comes out. I cherish that I can tell him anything, and he won't make me feel silly for describing how I feel.

It's important to empathize with what your spouse is feeling. It will help to maintain open communication lines. If they are judged or criticized every time they talk to you, it damages the relationship. Be more understanding and compassionate when talking to your spouse. It will strengthen the marriage.

Now, this does not mean you should never tell your spouse negative information. At the beginning of the chapter, I had to tell my husband I wanted him to help with the dishes. I didn't call him lazy and tell him he never helps me with anything. I used an "I" statement, which we learned to use in leadership classes. "I" statements focus on your thoughts and feelings and not criticizing the person's actions. It disarms the person by telling them how you are feeling.

A bad way to provide negative information to someone is by name-calling and yelling. You should not wait until you are mad or resentment has built up before you give negative feedback. The information may come out worse and cause the person to be defensive. Instead, wait until you are both calm and in a decent mood before providing any feedback. Again, focus on how you are feeling and not insulting your spouse.

My husband said I have gotten better at providing negative feedback over the years. He did not like that I repeated what I did not like multiple times during a conversation. I repeated it because he didn't react to the information. Once he told me he did not like me repeating it, I stopped. I realized I only needed to say something once, and he would get it. I appreciate him for letting me know. I did not comprehend how much it bothered him, and I didn't realize I was doing it.

In marriage, you will have awkward conversations. You should not avoid conflict. Things will actually get worse if you do. It is better to talk through issues and let your spouse respectfully know when things are bothering you. Again, having open communication will strengthen your relationship. It may be hard to receive negative feedback; still, listen carefully to your spouse's perspective and improve in areas where you can. You may not have realized that what you were doing is annoying.

Keep in mind, there is a line that needs to be drawn. I did not complain to my spouse about every little thing I did not like. I did not mention every single time he did not pick up after himself. I let a lot of little stuff go. God forgives me for all the wrong things I do regularly; therefore, I can forgive my husband for the little mistakes he makes. It can become unbearable if someone comes to you about every mistake you make. There has to be a balance. Yes, bring up the big issues to your spouse in a tactful way. No, don't be a faultfinder and complain about everything they do.

In the end, a happy marriage will still have awkward conversations. Ensure there are more positive exchanges where you share your thoughts and learn from each other's perspectives. Be supportive of your spouse. Maintain a marriage with open communication.

In the next chapter, I will discuss another time I had to have an awkward conversation with my husband.

Chapter 6

Tip #5: Show Appreciation

Early in our marriage, I did the dishes, cooked, and cleaned the house with no response from my husband. Within the first few weeks of being married, I finally told him I liked hearing, "thank you." Since then, my husband has been wonderful about showing appreciation when I cook, clean, or do an errand for him. It was a tough conversation to have, but I'm glad I told him. I have felt very appreciated throughout our 10-year marriage.

My husband told me he grew up in a household where his family hardly ever said, "Thank you." He said they showed appreciation in other ways, usually by doing favors for each other. Once he knew how important it was for me to verbally hear a "thank you," he started expressing gratitude more and more.

Now, I did not expect him to tell me, "Thank you," after everything I did for him. However, I did want to feel valued every now and then, but he has gone above and beyond to make me feel appreciated. He is continually showing his gratitude. One time he randomly said, "I've been noticing all of the things you've been doing for the family, and I appreciate it." *How sweet!*

Not every person needs to hear an occasional "thank you," but many do. According to a survey by author Shaunti Feldhahn for her book, *The Surprising Secrets of Highly Happy Marriages*, she learned that a guy feels the most cared for when his wife notices something he has done and sincerely thanks him for it. Her survey showed 72% of men said they were deeply impacted by being thanked for what they did.

In another book, *The All-or-Nothing Marriage: How the Best Marriages Work,* the author writes about the importance of expressing gratitude. Eli J. Finkel, Director of Northwestern University's Relationships and Motivation Lab, said a person's experience of gratitude predicts their partner's warm treatment towards them. If a partner starts to feel gratitude, it increases the other partner's positivity toward them, creating a cycle of mutual gratitude, kindness, and commitment.

Do you see how showing appreciation to your partner is vital to a happy marriage? One University of Georgia study even found that couples who showed higher gratitude levels to their spouses were less prone to seek a divorce. Researchers also found that partners feel appreciated and valued, impacting how they feel about their marriage.

While my husband said he does not need to hear, "Thank you," I still make sure I express gratitude for all he does for me. I thank him when he cuts the grass, watches the children while I nap, or when he does the dishes and cleans the kitchen. I don't want him to ever doubt that I value him as my husband. According to the other studies, it also turns out that showing him gratitude helps to make our marriage stronger.

It is easy to take your spouse for granted and not recognize everything they do for you. For example, if you have a stay-at-home spouse, that person probably does much of the household work. Don't neglect to thank them for activities such as cooking, keeping the house clean, doing the laundry, and watching the children.

If you have a working spouse, you can thank them for bringing home money to pay bills. I thanked my husband for working a double shift or overtime and adding more money to the household. It is not always easy to go to work every day, so I was grateful for my husband working extra hours.

If you are not regularly showing appreciation to your spouse, it is easy to begin strengthening your marriage. Suppose they are doing something daily that you can recognize or acknowledge. You may think it is their job to do what they are doing; however, that's not true. Your spouse does not necessarily have to cook, clean, take out the trash, or do the laundry. Be grateful for what they do and acknowledge their effort.

Consider this. At work, I have more respect for the bosses who regularly show appreciation. Yes, I am getting paid for the work I do. Still, it is nice to hear my boss, in particular, express gratitude. When they do not show appreciation to me and for my work, my morale and job satisfaction level are low.

The same way I feel unrecognized at work may be how your spouse is feeling at home. Their morale may be down, and the marriage's satisfaction level may be low as well. To turn things around, all you need to do is show your spouse appreciation regularly. It does not have to be with a "thank you." You can show gratitude in other ways, like buy them a gift, give them a break, or demonstrate affection. Just do something. Don't assume your spouse knows that you are grateful.

I like a quote from author William Arthur Ward. He said, "Feeling gratitude and not expressing it is like wrapping a present and not giving it." Your spouse cannot read your mind. Let them know how you feel. You might be like my husband, who says he does not need to hear "thank you." Just because you do not need to hear it does not mean your spouse does not need to. Instead of following your own preferences, act according to those of your spouse.

Many people do like to hear expressions of gratitude. As writer Gertrude Stein said,

"Silent gratitude isn't very much to anyone." When I work jobs where I do not feel appreciated, my level of effort sinks after a while. In a marriage where there is not much gratitude shown, spouses may feel the same way. A spouse may not try as hard to make the marriage work under those circumstances. They may feel exhausted from working so hard in the marriage and not being recognized or acknowledged. Don't let your spouse feel that way—express gratitude.

If you do not feel like expressing gratitude because your spouse never acknowledges you, take the high road. When you start showing appreciation to your spouse, it may cause them to show the same gratitude to you. If you both are not feeling appreciated, one of you has to make the first move. Once your spouse starts feeling appreciated, they will be more willing to send you positive vibes. It is such a small change to make to improve your marriage.

If you have children in the house, they will learn from your behavior. When I was growing up, I remember my mother saying, "Thank you" to everyone. She thanked the waiter for everything they did when we went out to eat. She thanked them for bringing out the drinks, bringing out the food, and providing good customer service. I remember her always telling anyone who did something for her, "Thank you." I started to do the same thing when I got older. I made sure I thanked people who did something nice for me. Your children are always watching you—model good behavior on how you treat your spouse.

Once you get started showing appreciation more, the easier it will become to do it all the time. Not only does my spouse feel good when I express gratitude, but I also start to feel good saying it. Showing gratitude helps me to recognize what an awesome spouse I have and fulfilling marriage. Give it a try. Let your spouse know how much you appreciate them.

In the next chapter, I reiterate something you can do to increase your marriage's satisfaction level.

Chapter 7

Tip #6: Share Household Chores

The kitchen was a mess. My husband and I had cooked dinner together. He made the hamburgers, and I made the sweet potatoes fries. Actually, he helped cut the fries, and I seasoned and baked them. My husband had already done the dishes several days in a row. I told him I would take care of them after working out on the elliptical in the basement.

When I finished my 20-minute workout, my husband had cleaned the kitchen and was finishing up the dishes. I was delighted. He was such a sweetheart; of course, I made sure I expressed my appreciation.

The next tip for having a happy marriage is to share household chores. You and your spouse can decide how to split the chores by your unique situation. Make sure the division is fairly even. Research shows that couples who strike the right balance in dividing tasks have happier marriages. One report from the Pew Research Center's Religious Landscape Study revealed that sharing household chores is "very important" to a successful marriage. More than half of married U.S. adults or 56%, both with and without children, agreed.

My husband and I first discussed chores during pre-marital counseling. The assistant minister had a worksheet for us to fill out about roles in the relationship. We discussed who was going to do what activity and wrote down a name next to each. I recently found the worksheet when cleaning out one of my drawers and was surprised to see how accurate our responses were from 10 years ago.

Most of the activities had "both" next to them. We had both next to grocery shopping activities, providing income, cooking, planning vacations, keeping the house neat, disciplining the children, dishes, cleaning, and laundry. We had my husband's name next to yard work and automobile care. We only had my name next to handling the finances, decorating the home, and initiating discussions about the relationship. Everything we wrote then is still true for us now. I liked that we agreed both would share most of the household chores from the beginning.

Although we agreed to share household chores during pre-marital counseling, I still panicked in the first few days of our marriage when I did the dishes for a few days in a row. I was afraid my husband really was not committed to us sharing those responsibilities. Initially, I was going to tell that story in this chapter, but I felt it was more of a communication issue. Once I communicated with my husband about how I was feeling, I learned he simply did not know how to use my dishwasher. He was still committed to dividing up the household work.

After 10 years of marriage, I definitely feel the work is evenly divided. My husband is the only one who does the yard work, and I only take out the trash if he is out of town. Everything else, we mostly share in the responsibilities. We both do the laundry, cook, clean, and take care of the children.

Depending on what's going on in our lives, one may do more of a certain activity. During one season of our lives, my husband read stories and tucked our daughters into bed every night because I nursed our son to sleep. No matter what season it is, there is always a balance. I always feel he does his share of the work for the household.

I know I am very blessed. I have heard of relationships where things are uneven. One spouse does most of the work around the house, with the other spouse rarely helping out. In our home, we ignore the stereotypes about which gender should be doing certain activities. Since we both work full-time, we share the work responsibility that needs to be done in our home.

I don't know how you should divide housework if one spouse works outside the home, and the other manages the household. However you decide to split it, make sure it feels even to you. It could be that the person who stays home does all of the chores, and the other spouse is responsible for bringing home the money.

Alternatively, a couple may decide that one spouse is so busy managing the house during the day that the working spouse still has to help out after work. It might not seem even if one spouse stays home all day watching television, and the house is still not clean, and there's no food on the table when the working spouse gets home, so there needs to be a balance. If both spouses work, of course, I support a shared responsibility.

If things are not even, the spouse who feels overworked may feel resentment and unhappiness. You should want your spouse to feel content. In a later chapter, I discuss wanting the best for your mate, so if you are the spouse who is not satisfied with how the work is divided, then you will need to have a conversation with your spouse to tell how you are feeling. They should want to make a change or changes. As I stated earlier, people are happier in marriages where the workload is shared.

I grew up in a household where both my parents worked and shared household chores. (Well, actually, when we got older, my brother, sister, and I shared the chores.) However, there were still times when I saw both of my parents helping out around the house.

I was glad when my husband agreed that he wanted to contribute evenly to our household as well. Since it was what I experienced growing up, I wanted that for me. I need to thank Match.com again for bringing him into my life. Growing up in church, I know some people have antiquated views about men and women's roles. Some people believe only one gender should do the cooking and cleaning. I can imagine how overwhelming that can be for one person.

I asked my husband why he did not mind helping out around the house. He said he too grew up doing chores around the house; he also wants to do his part. I think that's good to know for anyone looking for a spouse. If you want someone willing to share household responsibilities, find someone required to do chores at a young age.

Some people never had to do chores. Their parents did everything for them. They may expect you to do everything for them when you get married. It is wise to find your future spouse's views out beforehand. I'm glad my husband and I were able to discuss our roles during pre-marital counseling.

If you are dating someone and have different views on managing the household, that person may not be right for you. If the person believes you should do most of the work around the house, and it should be a shared effort, the person does not seem like a good match. The person will probably not change after marriage. You will feel animosity toward them because you want your spouse to do more around the house. It is better to avoid marrying someone who has different views from you.

There may be some of you who do not mind doing the majority of the household chores. If you are content with your arrangement, keep things the same. If there's something you want your spouse to help with more, let them know. You should feel comfortable going to your mate about your concerns.

All-in-all, there's no set way for how to divide housework evenly. It is up to you and your spouse. Some are formal about the chores and create a chart or calendar describing who does what chores and when. Others take turns. For instance, one person does the dishes one day, and the other person does the dishes the next. Some divide the chores based on the actual activity. Like, one spouse may handle the laundry, dishes, and vacuuming, and another may take out the trash, do yard work, and handle the finances. There's a variety of ways to split chores. Do what's best for you and your spouse.

My husband and I do not have a formal way to handle our chores. When work needs to be completed, it gets done by one of us initiating the activity. We don't have a schedule of when we do work. If the laundry needs washing, one of us will throw the clothes or towels into the washing machine. If one of the rooms needs cleaning, one of us cleans it. Sometimes we work together on the chores. We might both cook dinner together, or we might both clean a room together. It depends on the situation and who is available. Somehow it works out where we do not need to formalize doing chores. We are still evenly contributing to the household.

One important thing I learned is that if you share household responsibilities, you may do them differently. My husband does not fold the towels the same way I do. He does not wash dishes the same way. He does many things differently than I do. It does not matter. Getting the chores done; that's all that matters.

There was a time when I thought my husband should do things my way. Then I learned it meant I would have to do everything as it discouraged him from doing any tasks. I don't want the burden of doing all of the chores; I realized there is more than one way of doing things.

Sometimes I have learned tips from my husband on how to do a chore a better way. If you want help around the house, let your spouse do things their way. Don't control how the job gets completed; just appreciate the help. It will get annoying if your spouse has to do things exactly the way you do. They will not want to do the activity, and you will be upset that you are doing all of the work yourself.

There are other ways to not overburden one spouse with all of the chores. If your children are old enough, you can assign some duties to them. If you have enough money, you can hire someone. Most people don't love doing chores. You do them because they need to be done, but there are options, so one person is not overwhelmed.

The main idea about sharing in the household responsibilities is to make sure the work gets divided to make both of you comfortable. If one person feels overburdened, it will lead to bitterness and discontentment. It may cause one person to have negative feelings about the other person. Try to ensure things are fair. Sharing household chores evenly leads to happier marriages.

In the next chapter, I will discuss another area where sharing the work makes for a more pleasant experience for both you and your spouse. That area is with rearing the children.

Chapter 8

Tip #7: Unite on Rearing the Kids

My husband and I were in the doctor's office, waiting to finally see our baby for the first time. We had waited for the 8-week appointment after I had a positive pregnancy test. The nurse came in first and showed us the baby. I thought I noticed a look of concern on her face. She left the room soon after showing us the ultrasound. Then she said the doctor would be in shortly.

When the doctor came, he told us the fetus had died. The baby only measured 7-weeks old. He said I had a missed miscarriage. The baby died, but my body didn't know it. It caught us completely off guard. We had been trying for a few months to have a baby and were too excited when we finally got a positive pregnancy test. We called everyone in our families and told them about the baby.

Upon hearing the news, I didn't react immediately; I was still too shocked. It was my sister's wedding day, and I had slipped the doctor's appointment in the first thing that morning, so I didn't have to take two days of leave from work. In hindsight, that probably was not the best decision. I didn't have time to grieve right away. I spent the rest of the day focused on my sister's wedding. It was a good distraction, as I concentrated on making sure she had a wonderful marriage ceremony. It wasn't until that night when I was lying in bed that I let myself react.

Tears were pouring from my eyes. I told my husband I felt like I failed and had done something wrong. He said all of the right things. He reminded me that something was wrong with the baby. It wasn't anything I did. He also said, "You know we're going to keep trying."

That was what I needed to hear exactly. First, my husband did not blame me for losing the baby. Second, we were on the same page. We both wanted a baby. We were going to keep trying until we had one.

A few weeks later, my body officially miscarried. The next month I was pregnant. This time we waited until after the first trimester before telling anyone. Two trimesters later, we gave birth to a healthy baby girl.

The next tip on having a happy marriage is to unite on raising the kids. When you have children, all kinds of unplanned struggles and craziness happens. You have to connect and work on solving problems together. You may not have the same point of view, so you will need to have discussions to decide how to move forward together.

The first decision you have to agree on is whether or not you want children. Hopefully, you discussed this before getting married. Then you have to decide when you want to have children. I wanted them immediately, but my husband was not ready yet. I had to wait until he was comfortable, so we did not start trying until after four years of marriage. It's easier to rear children if both parents are ready to have a child.

When our daughter was born, I did not have a clue as to how to rear her. My husband had more experience than I did. He grew up with several nieces and nephews, so he was around babies more. We had many discussions on how we were going to parent our children.

We discussed whether to give our baby formula or to breastfeed. When the nurse said breastfeeding was free, we opted to nurse her. We did not have a long family history with breastfeeding. It was challenging at first. We had several visits from the lactation coach while in the hospital. I still did not know what I was doing when I left the hospital, so our pediatrician's office had me come in regularly for appointments.

Through it all, my husband was very supportive. He brought the baby to me in the middle of the night and tried to help me get her latched on. He kept encouraging me to keep trying. When I called the hospital's breastfeeding hotline, the lactation coach told me to stick with it for two weeks, and then it would get easier. She was right. After two weeks, our daughter and I knew what we were doing. I went on to nurse her for 14 months until we conceived our second daughter. Then I easily and exclusively breastfed my other two children for at least a year.

You definitely need a supportive partner to get through the trials of learning how to breastfeed. While I did all of the feedings, my husband mostly burped the babies and changed diapers. I don't think I changed our oldest daughter's diaper until two weeks after she was born. My husband had gone to a restaurant to pick us up some food when she had a dirty diaper. All other times, he changed her diaper. Just as you should divide and conquer the household chores, you should share the responsibilities of taking care of the children. Don't leave all or most of the duties to one spouse.

Sleep is a very big deal when you have a baby. In the hospital, my husband woke and handed the baby to me throughout the night to feed her. He stayed up with me at home in the middle of the night as I attempted to get her back to sleep. Then we would sleep when she slept during the day. When we had our second child, I only woke at night to feed her. I let him sleep. Then, in the morning, my husband would wake and take our first daughter to daycare and get us breakfast. He usually allowed me to rest during the day and get caught up on my sleep. He would watch the baby if she was awake.

In the beginning, that worked out well for us. We made sure we each got enough sleep. When we had our third child, I would again stay up in the middle of the night with him and nurse him back to sleep. My husband would take the other children to daycare. He often read a bedtime story to the girls before putting them to bed and woke up early with them on his days off. If either of us needed a nap during the day, one of us would watch all three children while the other took a nap. There was plenty of sharing the responsibility of child-rearing as not to be overburdened.

One topic we discussed before we had children was discipline. Although both of us got spanked when we were growing up, I was firmly against hitting our children. My husband was not totally against it. He used to be the disciplinarian with his nieces and nephews and was called to come and give them spankings. I had read about the effects on a child's brain and personality if they get spanked. I did not want to use physical violence to discipline our children.

My husband's first position was that spanking would be the last resort. He did not want to agree that he would never spank our children. I accepted his response. Instead of spanking, we would talk to our children about what they did and not hit them. So far, we have never hit our children. I appreciate my husband for agreeing that spanking would not be our go-to discipline. During our many discussions on the subject, he revealed he was worried our children might be out of control. They are still well-behaved without spankings, so I think it has reduced some of his fears.

Disciplining your children is notably a discussion you should have with your spouse. You need to be on the same page with what to do if your child starts misbehaving. I'm glad we had the discussion. There are times when our children make me angry, and it would be easy to hit them. However, since we decided that spanking is not the way to discipline, I have more self-control and find ways to calm down and not release my anger on our children.

When the children got a little older, they did try to play my husband and me against each other. I have learned to take his side and not go against something he said to them already. If I disagree with him, we talk privately, and I let him provide a different answer to the children if he changes his mind. He and I always try to have a united front with them. There are times when we didn't know the other spouse provided a different answer. When we find out, we tell the child to listen to their dad or mom. We want to make sure they all know we are a team.

While we are a team, rest assured, my husband and I don't do everything exactly the same. I usually drop the children off at daycare, and he picks them up. On Mondays, my husband is off work, so I let him get the children ready for daycare. At first, I stayed with him and helped the children before going to work. After a while, I decided to take advantage of him being home. I went to work early and got home early. I trusted him to get them ready.

I admit that I would help pick out outfits and do the girl's hair at night to prepare. Before long, the more my husband got the children ready by himself, the better he got at it. He used to call me asking about how to do things. Gradually, he did not need to contact me in the morning; he had his own way of getting them ready for daycare. I had my own way of doing things too, so I did not force my husband to do things the way I do them. (I discussed this in the *Share the Household Chores* chapter.)

All that mattered to me was that my husband got the children to daycare, and they looked decent. They would often tell me how "Daddy does things" when he picks them up or drops them off whenever it was my turn. I would tell them this is how "Mommy does it." They got used to following different patterns with each parent.

While we had different ways of doing things with our children, my husband and I still emphasized the same values. We believed the children should listen to their parents. We believed in keeping them safe, and we thought they are young and should have fun. Our children are more well-rounded because they experienced the styles of both parents implementing the same family values.

When my husband and I were first married, he wanted us to be more stable before starting a family altogether. We bought our house and made sure we had secure jobs before having children. Once he was ready, we were financially prepared and could afford children. I was impatient and wanted a family immediately. In hindsight, I agree with my husband's mindset. Rearing the children when we were financially able to do it, I think, made it less stressful for us. Also, our uniting in child-rearing made it easier.

Once we had our first child, we loved the idea of having more children. We had another one less than two years later. After having our second child, we both knew we wanted a third. The children were fun to play with, and kids really do say the darnedest things. Make sure you and your spouse feel the same way about having children (or more children). It will make the responsibilities of rearing them more manageable. Both you and your partner will also be more willing to unite.

While I know unplanned things happen, still have discussions with your spouse and try to get on one accord in rearing your children. You have nine months to prepare. Make sure both of you are involved in your child's life. Children need both of you. Having them is a blessing, so rear them with love, care, and unity.

Rearing children can take a lot of your time. You mustn't neglect your relationship with your spouse. In the next chapter, I will discuss how to keep a romantic relationship with your spouse strong throughout your marriage.

Chapter 9

Tip #8: Stay Affectionate

Our wedding planner was old-fashioned and knew all of the wedding etiquette rules. She told us things, such as how we should walk down the aisle, where we should stand during the ceremony, and how we should exchange wedding rings.

It was not until my husband was told to "kiss the bride" that I realized we did not discuss how to kiss during the ceremony with the wedding planner. So, I opened my mouth wide and French-kissed my husband. During the kiss, the photographer caught a photo of my brother, who was the minister marrying us, turning away.

I learned later that isn't how I was supposed to kiss my husband during the wedding. I was supposed to do more than a peck on the lips, but not a two-minute French kissing session. I was to show love to my husband without making our guests feel uncomfortable, according to etiquette expert Diane Gottsman, author of *Modern Etiquette for a Better Life*.

While the way I kissed my husband was a little too much for the wedding ceremony, affection is a good thing for a marriage. Research shows that showing affection during the marriage has positive effects on children and the relationship. A study published by the U.S. Department of Health and Human Services found that the quality of a couple's marriage has as much influence on a child's future mental and physical health as the child's own relationship with either parent.

Sometimes the passion at the wedding and the beginning of the marriage disappears. You mustn't let it, and you must maintain affection with your spouse throughout your relationship. Most people know it is essential to show love to your children. It is also crucial that you retain affection with your spouse. It is actually beneficial for your child to see a loving relationship with him or her.

Marriage is the most important relation-ship in any family, says David Code, author of *To Raise Happy Kids, Put Your Marriage First.* Code says couples should openly show affection to one another in front of the chil-dren. It will show them what a healthy rela-tionship and "healthy love" look like and help them feel safe and secure. Code recom-mends showing love by holding hands, hug-ging each other, and giving each other a quick kiss.

Without knowing the recommendation of relationship experts, my husband and I regularly show affection towards each other. We do not passionately kiss each other every day as we did at the wedding. Instead, we give a quick peck on the lips when we leave for work and when we return home.

My husband goes to work early in the morning. Usually, I am asleep when he is get-ting ready. Still, before he leaves, he leans over the bed and gives me a quick kiss on the lips. Then I go back to sleep. Sometimes, I ad-mit, I don't remember the morning kiss. I am in too deep of sleep to remember. If I talk to him on the phone during the day, I will ask him about the kiss. He always says I reacted to it even if I don't remember it happened.

When I have to work, and my husband doesn't, I make sure to kiss him in the morning before I leave for work. I always tell him I love him before I go. He does the same. The good thing about the morning kiss ritual is we always do it no matter what. If we have a little disagreement the night before, we still kiss each other the next morning. The kiss helps us get back on track, and things are usually normal again when we see each other later.

When we get home from work, we always greet each other with a kiss, hug, or both. The children are usually around to see us. Then they each want their own hug or kiss. We agree that the children seeing us be affectionate towards each other is healthy for them. Again, we do not do a full-blown make-out session. We give each other a quick peck on the lips and a tight hug. We keep it G-rated, as Amy McCready, parenting expert and Positive Parenting Solutions founder, suggests. She says not to act overtly sexual in front of your kids. It may make them feel uncomfortable or scared. However, simple signs of affection between parents can be comforting and reassuring to the children.

I will admit, when neither of us has to go to work, we sometimes forget to kiss first thing in the morning. We may share a kiss later during the day to make up for missing it. We also do more spontaneous displays of affection when we don't follow our usual routine.

Another routine we have is to hold hands when we're praying. When we're at church, we hold hands during every prayer. When we are watching online church, we sometimes hold hands when we are praying. If we're not sitting next to each other, we don't walk across the room to grab each other's hands. We simply hold hands when we are sitting next to each other. Also, when we are praying before a meal, we usually hold hands. That is a simple thing we do that connects us. Our routines ensure that we are touching each other every day. Staying affectionate throughout marriage keeps the feelings of intimacy alive.

With your relationship, continuously show affection toward your spouse. Kiss, hug, and hold hands with your spouse regularly. Develop your own routines so you will not neglect to show affection. Nurture your relationship daily. Frequently showing fondness to your spouse will remind them that you still love and care about them.

Keep this in mind; daily affection does not always have to be in the bedroom. Show simple affection outside the bedroom. It will let your spouse know you are not only affectionate when you want something from them in the bedroom. Bedroom intimacy is important too, and you should continue to exercise your rights as a married couple regularly. However, that should not be the only time you show affection towards each other. You should be able to hug, kiss, and holds hands publicly where your children can see your loving relationship, and your spouse knows you care for them aside from the bedroom.

When you neglect affection, it starts to seep into other areas of your marriage. Resentment starts to build up. For instance, you might begin to have less patience toward your spouse. You might also start to wonder how they feel about you. You might even wonder if they have feelings for someone else. Don't let your marriage begin to go down the wrong path. Continuously remind your spouse that you love and care about them. Show affection daily.

In the next chapter, I will discuss another way to show you support and care about your spouse.

Chapter 10

Tip #9: Be a Cheerleader

When I graduated with a master's degree in Journalism, I remember what my brother told me.

"Now, you'll never get married," he joked.

While he was teasing, I knew what he was implying. He was saying some men could not handle marrying someone who was highly educated or very successful. It might affect their sense of worth.

I could tell early on that my husband was not like that. He was actually the opposite. He wanted me to do well and reach my fullest potential. When we first met, I was not happy at my job. He encouraged me to apply for new ones and continually emailed me about new openings to the point where I started to get mad.

He kept sending me jobs that were $20,000 to $50,000 more than I was currently making. I asked him why he was sending me jobs out of my range, and he told me he didn't think it was out of reach for me. He said I could be making much more money with my master's degree. My husband had a high school diploma and was already making $14,000 more a year than me.

I started to think maybe it was possible to get a job that paid way more than I was making. I began to apply to the jobs my husband sent me. I found some of my own higher-paying jobs to apply to as well. Eventually, I did get hired for a job that paid $22,000 more than I was making. I appreciate my husband for believing in me. I had a limited mindset, and he believed I was capable of getting a higher salary.

The next tip to have a happy marriage is to be a cheerleader to your spouse. The definition of a cheerleader is someone who supports and praises. My husband is a constant source of encouragement. Whenever I doubt myself or fear doing something new, he always motivates me to keep going or do what I am afraid of doing. Having a spouse who is constantly in your corner makes marriage much easier.

A Carnegie Mellon University study found that people with supportive spouses were more likely to take on rewarding challenges, and those challenges led to more personal growth, happiness, psychological well-being, and better relationships. The study found that the most supportive partners expressed enthusiasm about opportunities and discussed the benefits of challenges.

My husband was supportive of me writing this book. I always wanted to tell our story. He encouraged me to write even when I doubted myself and reminded me that if our experiences can help someone's marriage, it is a success. I like that my husband motivates me to go beyond my self-imposed limits.

I can imagine how difficult it would be if you had a spouse who discourages you all of the time. You want to better yourself and get a new job, and your spouse tells you the grass is not greener on the other side. The spouse tells you you might not like the new position and to stay where you are. You want to get another degree or a new certification, and your spouse tells you it will be too hard for you. Living in a situation where someone is always doubting and discouraging you can be demoralizing. No one can live like that for too long.

If you don't want your spouse to be successful and to do better, it may be because of your own fears. You might be afraid of reaching the next level yourself, and you are projecting your fears onto your mate. You may also fear your spouse being more successful than you, and you believe you should be the most successful one in the relationship. Another fear you might have is if your spouse is too successful, they will leave you for someone else. Trying to hold someone back is not the right way to handle your fears. It will actually make things worse.

People know when someone genuinely supports them. If you are not supportive of your spouse, they might start to harbor negative feelings about you. Then they will be unhappy in the marriage, which will lead to your own unhappiness. The best marriages work when both partners are happy, thriving, and encouraging each other.

In the same way that my husband encourages me, I encourage him. There was a job opening he saw where he did not think he met the qualifications. I encouraged him to apply for it. He got the job, which was a raise on what he was currently making. It also came with an automatic raise for the next two years. If I did not motivate him to apply to the job, he would have never been chosen for it and got a significant pay increase.

Couples need to support each other and be each other's best cheerleaders—my husband cheers for me when I get promotions, raises, and awards. I can feel his genuine praise for me. I congratulate him when he also gets raises, bonuses, and promotions. As I said in the *Put Money Together* chapter, when one of us does well, the entire family does well.

Since we continue to encourage each other, my husband has doubled his income since we first met. I have tripled mine because I started with a salary way lower than him. Our current income is pretty much around the same amount, but we're not competing. We are on the same team. It is easy to cheer for someone who is in your corner.

As mentioned earlier, you should not think of your spouse as your competition but as your partner or teammate. Praise them when they do well. Motivate them to go for the promotion; encourage them to pursue their goals. When your spouse is fulfilled, they have more zeal to commit to the marriage's overall well-being.

I have always been very ambitious. I did well in school and always wanted to climb the ladder in my career. I am thrilled that I married someone who does not mind if I pursue my goals. I don't need to shrink for my husband. I can be my go-getter self and not worry about it bothering him.

Not only does my husband cheer me on in the pursuit of my goals, but he also encourages me when things go wrong. He was supportive when I didn't get promotions or when I had a bad day at work. He comforted me when loved ones died and provided me a shoulder to lean on.

We have a mutually supportive relationship. We support each other through difficult times. I was also there for my husband when he didn't get the promotions he wanted. We encourage each other to keep trying when things don't go our way. We remind each other to trust in God and that everything will work out.

We also followed the advice to not try to fix our spouse's problem. Sometimes we just serve as a listening ear to let each other vent and talk through issues. We showed each other that we have faith in each other. If we did not get a promotion, we reassured each other we would get one eventually. It has helped us to get through challenging situations quickly instead of dwelling in difficult times.

We motivate each other to move forward and not to stay upset too. Our interactions are uplifting. Many people in the world criticize, belittle, or try to bring people down. I had supervisors who expressed a lack of confidence in my abilities. If I am not careful, I may start to believe other people's negative comments about me. It's good to have someone at home who supports me and builds me up. It helps me to ignore people who do not believe in me.

You should provide the same support for your spouse. Be someone who encourages your spouse and not someone who lowers their self-esteem. Your house should be a safe haven for your spouse, where they receive love and support. Don't contribute to their negativity at work or even with friends and family members. Empower and lift them up.

I know there are many marriages where the spouse is the person who helps destroy a person's sense of self-worth. It should not be that way. Your spouse should be one of the most supportive people in your life. If they aren't, find out why and what needs to change. Let them know how you are feeling and what they can do to be more supportive. If you are not supportive of your spouse, shift how you interact with them. It's not too late.

According to the Journal of Personality and Social Psychology, spouses reporting greater partner support are more satisfied with their marriages than those reporting less support. I have seen celebrities who do exceptionally well or have outstanding achievements, and then there is a divorce.

While I don't specifically know what went wrong in those marriages, I know it helps to have a partner support you during good times and bad. It's not right to have a partner who supports you during bad times but is jealous of you during good times. You need a happy spouse when you are successful and one who mourns with you when you are sad.

Support your spouse in merry and in miserable times. Be their cheerleader. The next chapter has one final tip for having a happy marriage.

Chapter 11

Tip 10: Put Your Spouse First

During the first conversation with my spouse, after I had discovered him on Match.com, we were trying to decide what restaurant to meet at for our first date. I could have named a steakhouse or a costly restaurant. Instead, I agreed to go to Chili's Grill & Bar, where it had a two for $20 deal, including an appetizer and a dessert. I thought if we were not a good match for each other, I did not want him to waste too much money on us when he could better spend it on bills or something else. I know another couple that met online and has been married for more than 15 years. They had their first date over coffee. They did not have to go to an expensive restaurant on their first date either.

I know people who have a different point of view of those mentioned above. They want to take advantage of their date by choosing one of the most expensive items on a menu since someone else is paying, while others like their date to prove their worth by spending extra money on them. I was not thinking like that. I was thinking about what would be best for him. In that instance, it was to not allow my date to spend beaucoup money on someone he did not know yet.

While we were only dating back then, I think the same way now that we are married. I am continually thinking about what I can do to make his life better. I want what's best for him. I avoid doing things that will hurt him or make things worse. That leads me to the final tip.

The last tip for a happy marriage is to put your spouse first. The advice is pretty much a summary of all of the recommendations, which may be a little controversial. I have a disclaimer so you can better understand. This tip works best when you follow the first tip, *Choose the Right Person*. It won't work as well if you marry a selfish person. That person will take advantage of your kindness. Your efforts will never balance. You need to heed my warning and marry someone as kind and considerate as you are.

The way this tip is set up, I am always looking out for my husband's well-being. I do not flirt with other guys or cheat on him because I want what's best for him. I communicate openly to him because he must know how I am feeling. I put my money together with his so we could both be debt-free and financially stable. It even shows up when I don't let things get too lopsided in our relationship by sharing household chores and parenting our children with him. I know that if things get skewed, it will cause me to resent him, which won't be good for the relationship.

I also watch all of our children while he takes a nap because I know he needs rest. I attend work functions with him because I know it is good that his wife is present. I don't call him names that disrespect him because that will tear him down, not build him up. I am available physically for him because I know he has his needs.

While I am meeting my husband's needs, it is evident that he puts me first, too. One of my favorite things he does is put gas in my car. The gas station we go to is not on my way to work, and whenever I tell him I have to get gas before coming home, he says to come home, and he will put gas in my car. One time he said he didn't want his wife standing in the cold to get gas; I love that! It shows he cares for me and wants what is best for me.

My husband does some of the things I do for him as well. He wakes up early with the children and lets me sleep in sometimes. He also watches all of our children during the day and allows me to get a nap. *Can you tell how important sleep is to me?* I know he does not love doing chores, but he does them because he is looking out for me. Likewise, he expresses his appreciation for me *to me* because he knows that's what I want to hear.

With him looking out for me and me focusing on his needs, we have a happy marriage. We both want what's best for each other. It balances out when I put my spouse first because he is putting me first.

Now I know some church people reading this book are thinking you should not put your spouse first; you need to put God first. You are absolutely correct. Of course, God should be first in your marriage. You should strive to live a life that is pleasing to God first. I'm just saying this *Put Your Spouse First* advice is about putting your spouse before yourself. Consider how your actions will affect them. Find ways to do things that benefit one another, and avoid doing things that will adversely affect your spouse.

You may have the urge to put yourself first in your marriage and not worry about your mate. This is what it might look like. You flirt with members of the opposite sex or cheat on your spouse because it feels good to you. It ends up destroying your spouse and ruining your marriage. Perhaps you let your spouse do all of the housework, and you treat them like your servant. They are stressed out and unhappy in the marriage. The spouse might even look outside of the union for someone more thoughtful. You might even yell mean things to your spouse when you are arguing. It starts to diminish the love they have for you.

As you can see from those three examples, putting yourself first without considering your mate does not end up working well for you. It may have immediate benefits and you may feel good telling your spouse off or seeking revenge for something they did. You may also enjoy being lazy and not helping out around the house. However, it slowly starts to damage your marriage in the long run, which will also negatively affect you.

If you usually look out for yourself first, try to focus on your spouse and do things to please them. You will be surprised how much easier things will get for you. If your marriage has already gone down the wrong path, you might be hesitant to focus on your mate. You might think they don't focus on your needs and wonder why you should focus on theirs. Give it a chance. Try putting your spouse first for about a month. Communicate openly with them using kind words. Participate in activities they enjoy. Notice the positive things they do and express your appreciation.

Your spouse should notice the change and may want to reciprocate. It will change the trajectory of the relationship. Instead of tension, there will be peace. Eventually, you will realize it is better to consider their needs before doing something that offends them.

If you feel like you are already the one who sacrifices for your spouse, keep doing it for another month. Look for ways you are not putting them first and fix it. If you have negative thoughts about your spouse, shift to positive ones. You might be surprised how that little action will change the way you interact with them. Your change in interaction will probably lead to your spouse reacting more positively to you. If, after a month, your spouse has still not changed and is putting themselves first, communicate how you feel. They may not know. If there is still no change, you have to set boundaries.

As I mentioned at the beginning of this chapter, you may have a selfish spouse. You cannot let them walk all over you—set boundaries on what you will accept, as mentioned in the *Get Pre-marital Counseling* chapter. Do not allow your mate to go beyond those boundaries without you peacefully communicating with them.

Give the month challenge a try. Don't declare your spouse a selfish person without actually trying a month of focusing on his or her needs. You might not notice the unfriendly vibes you are letting seep out. When there is conflict, spouses tend to blame each other for them and not see their part. Even if you have a minor role in the clash, try to fix your part to see if things get better. If not, set boundaries. I have had to in other relationships besides marriage, which was very effective in improving the relationship.

Ultimately, the best situation would be if you are in a happy, loving marriage. However, you cannot change the other person. You can only change yourself. One way to initiate change is to put your spouse first. Do what you are supposed to do. In most circumstances, it will lead to your spouse wanting to treat you the same positive way.

When you are in a happy marriage, it makes everything better. I gave several tips in this book to have a happy marriage. This tip sums up all of the other ones. If you are not sure what action to take to improve your relationship, put your spouse first. It may lead to everything else, falling into place in your marriage.

Conclusion

You have read 10 things my husband and I did to enjoy a happy union. If you are not married yet, you can build a strong foundation for when you get married. Out of all of the advice I gave, my best advice is to **marry the right person**. Billionaire Warren Buffet agrees. In HBO's 2017 documentary, "Becoming Warren Buffet," he says the most significant decision of your life will be who you choose to marry. He credits his first wife, who has since died, for his success. "What happened with me would not have happened without her."

If you are married, it is not too late for you to have a happy marriage. If you are having difficulties with the relationship, it does not necessarily mean you married the wrong person. I don't know your particular situation to tell you which of these tips you should implement to turn your marriage around, but consider which tips you are currently not doing and apply those practices. Be patient after you introduce a new method. Change does not happen overnight.

Continue to take steps in the right direction and avoid going back to your old ways. If you do make a mistake, it is okay. Commit to getting back on track and implementing tips toward having a happy marriage.

I wanted to end this book by mentioning my faith again. I give credit to God for blessing me with an awesome husband. I prayed for someone like him, and God answered my prayers. Marriage has been very easy because I am with the right person. Again, I am grateful to Match.com for introducing us. If you are single, I pray that you, too, will *meet your match.* If you are married, I pray some of the tips mentioned helps to revitalize your marriage.

About the Author

D Dee Dee Patterson is a wife and mother with three children who are all under 6 years old. Before she met her husband, she was frustrated, disappointed, and scared that her dream of being a wife and mother would never come to fruition. One day she did a very specific search on Match.com for her dream guy. She got one result! After contacting the man, they dated for a year before getting married. She has been married for over a decade and is in a happy and loving marriage after meeting her husband online. Besides writing this book, she blogs about going from dating to her dream life as a wife and mother at www.deedeepatterson.com.

Made in the USA
Middletown, DE
15 June 2021